BOOKS

and

BOMBS

JOSEPH H. DOENGES

Gotham Books

30 N Gould St.
Ste. 20820, Sheridan, WY 82801
https://gothambooksinc.com/

Phone: 1 (307) 464-7800

Published by Gotham Books (August 18, 2022)

ISBN: 978-1-956349-46-7 (sc)
ISBN: 978-1-956349-47-4 (e)

TABLE OF CONTENTS

*To the Faithful Companions of Jesus (FCJs)
throughout the world as they carry out the mission and
pursue the vision of their foundress,
Marie Madeleine d'Houët*

PREFACE

The purpose of this book is to document the events surrounding the terror attacks of September 11, 2001, as they unfolded in Waterloo, Belgium, at Saint John's International School. What happened that day in New York, Washington, D.C., and Pennsylvania had far-reaching consequences that disrupted lives throughout the world. As an international school serving primarily the expat community in the greater Brussels area, Saint John's experienced a shock that made everyone feel vulnerable. The ripple effect of what happened in the United States crossed the Atlantic almost instantaneously. The following pages attempt to capture the events that played out and the mood that existed in the aftermath of the worst terror attack on American soil. Hopefully this book will serve as a historical record of what happened that day from the unique perspective of the international school community in Waterloo, Belgium.

The notes for this book were compiled in the aftermath of September 11, but not reviewed and prepared for publication until thirteen years afterward. The primary format is based on a daily chronology of events as they unfolded hour by hour and day by day. It is certainly possible that the exact time of day referenced in the text could be off by minutes or even hours. Precision is sometimes a victim of memory. Nevertheless, the following pages contain no fiction whatsoever. All of the names mentioned are real. In some instances, opinions are rendered as I attempt to analyze the situation and draw conclusions. However, this is a true story.

ACKNOWLEDGMENTS

I am grateful to countless number of staff, students, and parents with whom I worked during a decade at St. John's International School. For a professional educator, such an experience was as good as it gets. The families came from all over the world to represent their home countries diplomatically or to pursue international business. The school was a melting pot of cultures, traditions, languages, and even religions. The result was a unique environment yielding an ethos of cooperation, tolerance, and respect that crossed all social, ethnic, and national boundaries.

INTRODUCTION

My wife, Martha, and I moved from Boerne, Texas, to Waterloo, Belgium, in July 1998. I assumed the role of high school principal at St. John's International School after serving as superintendent of schools in Boerne for the previous eleven years. One might wonder why anyone would move from the superintendency of a school district with more than four thousand students and five campuses to the principalship of a high school with fewer than three hundred. The answer was simply that it was the right time for change in our lives. Furthermore, we could not pass up the opportunity to live and work in Europe with staff and students from all over the world. St. John's enrolled more than nine hundred children, pre-kindergarten through high school, in meeting the needs of the expat community in Belgium. The Americans constituted the largest block with one-third of the enrollment, but children came from sixty different countries, including such far-flung destinations as Nepal, South Korea, Bangladesh, Eritrea, and South Africa. English was the language of instruction, but French was the compulsory second language for everyone.

The Faithful Companions of Jesus (FCJs), who started the school in 1964, did so in response to requests from the international business community to offer an English-based education with a Christian ethos. The nuns were already operating schools throughout the world, including a campus next to the convent in Brussels. They started the school with an emphasis on Christian values, but with an openness to students of all religious traditions. The original student body was limited to elementary age, but the response was so great that the school was soon relocated from Brussels to Waterloo, where the sisters had a summer home. Over the years, the enrollment continued to grow, and more grades were added. Eventually the FCJs collaborated with the De La Salle Christian Brothers at St. John's College High School in Washington, D.C., to staff and administer the high school. Today St. John's is under lay leadership. The brothers are no longer involved, and the sisters' role has been reduced to one of governance on the Board of Trustees.

It was in this international educational environment that I was happily serving as school director when the terror attacks of September 11, 2001 occurred in the United States. These infamous events took place on the other side of the Atlantic Ocean and six time zones removed from Europe. Nevertheless, their impact reached Belgium almost immediately, and we found ourselves in a fog of uncertainty, wondering what to do to protect our students and staff. St. John's was a school under possible siege and threat. We were a soft target with hundreds of vulnerable children. Hence the title, *Books and Bombs*

CHAPTER 1

The Setting

Waterloo is seventeen kilometers southeast of Brussels in northern Wallonia, the French-speaking part of Belgium. It had a population of about twenty-five thousand in 2001, almost a third of that being non-Belgian. Many of these expats worked in the diplomatic community, as Belgium hosted the European Union and the North Atlantic Treaty Organization, in addition to the normal representation associated with the Kingdom of Belgium itself. Others worked in the international business community, as many corporations had European offices in the area. Proctor and Gamble had been one the first companies to support St. John's and use the school to educate its dependent children. IKEA had its offices a mere five hundred meters from the school and sent many of its children there.

The fame of Waterloo, however, was established some two hundred years ago when Napoleon's French

Army was defeated just south of town by the Duke of Wellington and his British forces allied with the Dutch and the Prussians. The Battle of Waterloo took place on June 18, 1815, and has been memorialized in the chronicles of history ever since. Pop culture has even capitalized on this epic event with familiar songs such as "Waterloo" by the famous Swedish music group ABBA and another song bearing the same title by the American country singer Stonewall Jackson. The Battle of Waterloo was fought a mere five kilometers from St. John's International School, and the monument with the Lion of Flanders on top is visible from the third floor of the middle school wing.

The city of Waterloo is administered from a beautiful and modern "maison communal" located in the downtown area, one block from the main street. All of the city offices are housed in this large complex, including the police department, the department dealing with the registration of foreign residents, and the recreational facilities with a pool, tennis courts, and gym. The long-serving mayor was Serge Kubla, who was a strong supporter of St. John's. He was good friends with Sr. Barbara Hughes, FCJ, who had already been serving as the St. John's superintendent for eighteen years when we arrived. His "right-hand man" was one of the councilmen, the "premier échevin," Yves Vander Cruysen. Yves, too, was a strong supporter of St. John's and good friends with Sister Barbara, as well as with Nadine Tyteca, her, and later, my administrative assistant. These relationships were vital to the status of St. John's in the Waterloo community and later invaluable as the events described herein played out under stressful conditions.

The city of Waterloo was relatively wealthy by overall Belgian standards. There were many upscale retail stores, numerous excellent restaurants, and several nice hotels. Most of the locals commuted to jobs in Brussels, worked in the local shops, or were employed in a large business park that included the MasterCard European offices, IKEA, and a couple of major banks. It was a child-friendly environment for both the Belgians and the expats, who were drawn to the high standard of living and the presence of St. John's. There was also a Scandinavian School with several hundred students. It catered specifically to the educational needs of families from the Nordic countries.

The only real negatives for Waterloo were the traffic and the weather. These drawbacks, however, were Belgium-wide and not characteristic of any one location. Driving and parking were difficult for anyone with a vehicle, especially at rush hour. The rail line and buses into Brussels helped, but almost everyone experienced the frustration of bumper-to-bumper traffic jams and difficult-to-find parking spaces.

The weather, meanwhile, was dominated by rain. Temperature extremes were not unusual. It would often freeze in the winter, but rarely was there long-lasting bitter cold. In the summer, it would occasionally reach into the mid-thirties on the Celsius scale (mid-nineties Fahrenheit), and everyone would complain about the oppressive heat. Such complaints were indeed justified in an environment where air conditioning was not common since it was so rarely needed.

The rain, however, was famous. On average, it would rain almost every other day. A week without rain would constitute a dry spell, and a month with daily rain would not be unusual. Normally such precipitation was light, with heavy rains drenching the area on an occasional basis. Overall, the annual rainfall would average about 820 millimeters, or 32 inches. Nevertheless, the perception was that rain was a constant partner in learning to live comfortably in Belgium. Seattle, Washington has a similar climate in the United States. Everyone owned several umbrellas. Snow was not a common event in the winter, but it did occur virtually every season, sometimes on multiple occasions. It would usually melt in a day or two. Despite the weather issues, nothing could be more beautiful than a warm, sunny day in Belgium with the green fields and colorful flowers everywhere.

My first two years as high school principal were wonderful. I was able to enjoy the challenges of administering a small high school and getting to know the students on a personal basis while being sheltered from above by Sr. Barbara. I happily dealt with the kids, the parents, the teachers, and the coaches while she handled the board members, the finances, and relationships with the embassies, corporations, and city of Waterloo.

In the fall of 1999, Sr. Barbara announced her intention to retire at the end of the school year in June. I was in the right place at the right time with the right experience. The Board asked me to follow Sr. Barbara, and I reluctantly, yet happily, agreed to do so. The reluctance was due to the comfort that I enjoyed as high school principal. Why would I want to give up such a great job? The happiness was due to the feeling that the position was the "right fit" for me. The challenge of leading an established international school with such a great reputation was very attractive. So I followed Sr. Barbara upon her retirement. At the time of the transition, the Board changed the title of the top leadership position from superintendent to director, apparently thinking that the new terminology would be better with the school having a lay chief administrator for the first time.

CHAPTER 2

Events that Changed the World

The history of mankind has been shaped by momentous events that changed human civilization dramatically. Some of these milestone events were catastrophic and due to natural causes, some were inspirational and driven by the force of personality and genius, and some were traumatic and caused by the ever-present flaws in the human condition. It is probably easier to agree on a top ten than a top one hundred when considering such world-changing events. It must also be acknowledged that a list of such events would most likely reflect cultural and geographical differences. What is considered to be historically important in Japan may not resonate in Europe. What matters to South Africans may not register with North Americans. Nevertheless, there are those events that have had global impact and almost universal awareness of that impact.

The destruction of Pompeii by the eruption of Mount Vesuvius in AD 79 was certainly a catastrophe due to natural causes. Meanwhile the meltdown of three nuclear reactors in Fukushima, Japan, in 2011 is a more recent example of catastrophe caused by natural causes. The tsunami that destroyed the power plant was itself caused by an earthquake. Both events changed history, but their impact was more localized than global, especially Pompeii, which remained covered in twenty feet of lava and ash, only to be discovered more than a thousand years later. Fukushima probably would have suffered a similar fate had events there occurred before the development of nuclear energy and before photography, television, smart phones, and the Internet.

Milestone events inspired and driven by the force of personality and genius would certainly include the birth, life, death, and resurrection of Jesus. For Christians worldwide, this would be considered the most important event in the history of mankind. For nonbelievers, it would still have major impact because of the way the world has changed over the past two thousand years with the spread of Christianity. Likewise, Muhammad altered history with his teachings and the subsequent spread of Islam. Even those who do not consider him to be a prophet acknowledge his impact on the world starting in the sixth century and carrying forward to modern times. A more recent example of the force of personality and genius is Nelson Mandela, who spent twenty-seven years in prison prior to his release and subsequent election as the first black president of South Africa in 1994. By dismantling apartheid and establishing democracy, he was primarily responsible for historical change that will be more thoroughly measured in the decades and centuries to come.

Unfortunately, traumatic events that altered history are all too numerous. Many are rooted in military conquest. Others, although not militarily related, involve horrific violence. The Battle of Waterloo has already been mentioned as the site where European boundaries and even languages were altered by the Duke of Wellington's victory over Napoleon. The British, Dutch, and Prussians won; the French lost. It is easy to imagine what might have been if Napoleon had won and continued marching north. Constantine won the Battle of Milvian Bridge in AD 312 and attributed his success to the cross of Jesus. The result was his conversion to Christianity and its acceptance throughout the Roman Empire. The Spanish Armada was defeated in 1588 by British and Dutch forces, thus securing

Protestantism in the United Kingdom and control of the seas for Great Britain. The British Commonwealth as we know it today would probably not exist were it not for the defeat of the Spanish fleet. Hitler's rise to chancellor of Germany in 1933 was a prelude to World War II, the Holocaust, the death of millions, and the dramatic alteration of political boundaries. The atomic bomb dropped on Hiroshima in 1945 killed tens of thousands and revealed the devastation of nuclear weapons.

Not every dramatic event that changed history was based in natural disaster, the force of personality, or violence. Sometimes world-altering events were simply the result of luck, whether it be serendipity or preparation meeting opportunity. Christopher Columbus discovered a new world in 1492 while trying to reach India by sailing west from Spain. Today hundreds of millions speak Spanish as a result of his journey on behalf of King Ferdinand and Queen Isabella. Louis Pasteur captured the essence of preparation meeting opportunity with his comment in 1854 that "In the field of observation, chance favors only the prepared mind." His legacy is captured in the process of pasteurization and in the science of vaccination and microbial fermentation. The result is a better, safer, and healthier world where millions of lives are no longer lost routinely to disease and infection.

All of this brings us to the focus of this book: the Al Qaeda terror attacks of September 11, 2001. Four commercial aircraft were hijacked for the purpose of launching kamikaze-style attacks in the United States. American Airlines Flight 11 was flown into the North Tower of the World Trade Center in New York City at 8:46 a.m. United Airlines Flight 175 was flown into the South Tower at 9:03 a.m. Shortly thereafter at 9:45 a.m., American Airlines Flight 77 smashed into the Pentagon in Arlington, Virginia, just across the Potomac River from the nation's capital in Washington, D.C. At 10:10 a fourth aircraft, United Airlines Flight 93, crashed in a field near Shanksville, Pennsylvania. It never reached its likely intended target of the White House after passengers stormed the cockpit in an effort to reverse the hijacking.

Within hours, the twin towers collapsed into a heap of rubble as hundreds of millions watched on television throughout the world. Over three thousand were killed, including more than four hundred police and firefighters who had come to the rescue of thousands trapped inside. The United States went into a collective lockdown as all flights throughout the country were canceled and the military went on full alert. President Bush was in Florida visiting an elementary school when he received the news. Because of the uncertainty of what was happening, he left the school, but his plane was rerouted as far west as Oklahoma before eventually returning to Washington. The government went into crisis management. The country went into shock and mourning. The world was stunned.

The immediate impact was the realization that commercial air travel was vulnerable to terror attack. A subsequent series of letters containing anthrax sent through the postal system added to the sense of unchecked terrorism. Security became an obsession, and the security industry went into boom mode. Virtually every airport in the world implemented procedures to screen passengers and check luggage. Flight marshals were added to many U.S. flights. Security cameras were installed with the same frequency as outside lighting.

Without a doubt, the events of September 11, 2001, changed the world. It was another example of violence altering the course of history, much like the nuclear bombs dropped on Hiroshima and Nagasaki. This time, however, the ability to capture the violence as it occurred and televise it globally touched the entire planet. All those traveling today by air to any destination in the world are reminded of September 11, 2001, as they empty their pockets, take off their shoes, and pass through a metal detector before boarding a plane. The changes, however, were not limited to air travel. The remainder of this book describes events in Waterloo, Belgium, in the hours and days following September 11.

CHAPTER 3

September 11, 2001

It was a typical Tuesday in the first month of a new school year. More than one thousand students were engaged in learning activities. Lunch was finished, and the food service staff were cleaning up the cafeteria. A group of elementary-age children were enjoying recess on the playground. A few high school students were lounging on what was called "C-level," an activity area on the third floor next to the principal's and counselor's offices. The weather was typical for that time of year with intermittent rain showers interspersed with sunshine and partly cloudy skies. It was 12 degrees Celsius (54°F).

The drama began as the school's management team was gathered for its regular weekly meeting. Elementary school principal, Sr. Beatrice Molyneux,

FCJ; middle school principal, Mandy Macleod; high school principal, Dr. Nick Miller; business manager, Rick Katherman; and special education coordinator, Evelyn Keyes, were all seated around a conference table in the administrative villa. The administrative offices were located directly across the street from the school in a two-story chalet-style home with about eight hundred square meters of gardens and lawn surrounding it. The ground floor contained the director's office, secretary's office, admissions office, conference room, kitchen, and two restrooms. Upstairs were the business office, personnel office, and a restroom. There was a zebra-stripe crosswalk with a push-button stop light on Dréve Richelle, the busy street that separated the campus from the villa. The crosswalk and stop light were used many times a day by staff members going to the villa from the main campus and by hundreds of students who walked to school.

About an hour into our meeting, someone started pounding on the door to the conference room. I remember everyone looking up with startled expressions as Judith Hoskins, director of admissions, opened the door and blurted out, "Something terrible has happened. A plane has flown into a building in New York. Hundreds of people are dead." We were stunned and sat there without moving or saying a word as Judith started to cry. After several more seconds of awkward silence, we adjourned the meeting. The principals returned to their schools, each of which occupied a separate wing of the overall campus. I hurried across the street to the secondary school library, where we had a cable connection that provided access to numerous television stations, including CNN and Sky News.

By the time I arrived three minutes later, Cheryl Bruns, the middle and high school librarian, had tuned a television to one of the news channels. Several teachers who did not have students at that moment were also there watching the news reports from New York. It was fascinating video, and we were all mesmerized while watching constant replays of the crash. Shortly after 3:00 p.m. our time, another plane flew into the South Tower of the World Trade Center. At first we thought that it was simply another replay from a different camera angle, but then we realized that it was a second plane. Suddenly it was dramatically clear that this was no accident and that the United States was under attack. I thought of Pearl Harbor and the newsreels that showed the attacking Japanese planes and the sinking American naval vessels.

It was now very obvious that a major terror attack was under way in the United States. My immediate thoughts and priority were to keep the last half hour of the school day as normal as possible and to get the buses rolling after school in order to clear the campus. About 40 percent of the students rode a bus to and from school, while the rest of them either walked home or were picked up in cars by parents. The bus riders were transported on twenty-one vehicles that covered most of the area in the southeast quadrant from the center of Brussels. They ranged from large double-decker buses with a maximum capacity of seventy-two to smaller minivans that transported as few as eight. About five minutes before the dismissal bell, I went outside to the bus loading area, as I routinely did almost every day. The buses and vans were parked and ready to go. The drivers seemed totally unaware of what was happening in the United States. They were either standing around chatting casually or sitting in their vehicles and reading the newspaper. The bells sounded, and the older students streamed out of the buildings and started to board. The younger ones were led out by the classroom teachers to ensure that they boarded the proper bus. It was obvious that few, if any, of the children knew what was happening in the United States. The normal horseplay and laughter were on display as the kids boarded. At 3:45 I signaled the driver of the lead bus to go, and he was immediately followed by the others in a steady stream down Champ du Roussart, the narrow road behind the school, to the traffic circle on Dréve Richelle.

I felt a sense of relief knowing that the buses were gone and the vast majority of the other children had also departed. There were still a hundred or so students hanging around, but these were mainly athletes getting ready for volleyball or soccer practice. It was now time to try to figure out what was happening and determine what to do next. We had made no general announcement to the students and staff during the last half hour of school, as there was no intercom system with which to do so. Nevertheless, word of mouth traveled quickly, and most staff members seemed to be aware of the news as I walked back inside to the secondary library to get an update from the television news. Almost immediately the news shifted from New York to Washington, and it was being reported that a third plane had just crashed into the Pentagon in Arlington, Virginia. Suddenly my angst reached a whole new level of tension as I wondered about the safety of my son Karl, who was working in the Commerce Department, less than half a mile from the White House.

I stood in the library office area watching the television with a small group of teachers. The newscasters announced that the Federal Aviation Administration had canceled all flights in the United States and that President Bush had not yet returned to Washington from Florida because of concerns for his safety. The video images of the two planes crashing into the World Trade Center were played over and over again. Occasionally the news anchors would cut away to reporters on location in New York and Arlington, Virginia. Suddenly the South Tower of the World Trade Center started to implode and collapse before our eyes on global television. It was 9:59 a.m. in New York and 3:59 p.m. in Belgium. This added a new image to the constant replay cycle. Minutes later it was announced that another passenger plane had crashed in a field in rural Pennsylvania. At that point I realized that I was a spectator to history in the making, and it became frighteningly clear that I had a responsibility to ensure the safety of the St. John's community.

It was 4:15 p.m. when I climbed the stairs from the library, which was on the ground level, and walked down the corridor of the high school on what was known as B-level. Most of the mathematics classes were taught on this level, and a few students were being tutored as I hurried along, turned left into the fourth- and fifth-grade wing, and then exited the building to cross Dréve Richelle in order to get to my office in the villa. As soon as I walked in, Nadine Tyteca, the administrative secretary, gave me a message to call the American Embassy. I immediately phoned, and Mike Valle answered. Mike was the embassy security officer and also a St. John's parent. His daughter, Nicole, was in kindergarten. Hence, his interest in advising us was not just professional. It was personal as well.

Mike wanted me to know that the embassy staff and he were working feverishly to try to find out what was going on and that I could contact him at any time with questions. He commented that, even though the violence so far had been in the United States, it could not be ruled out that the terror attacks were part of a global conspiracy. He also mentioned that there was the danger of a copycat attack in Belgium because of the large American presence. St. John's was an international school, not an American school or a Department of Defense school. However, the highest percentage of students, about a third, were from the United States, and the American Embassy was the largest client. Mike promised to call again in about an hour.

At this point it was useless to sit in the office and wait for phone calls. So I went back across the street and methodically walked through all of the buildings, floor by floor and wing by wing, including Timber Tops, which was the preschool complex across the street behind the main campus. Everything was as normal as could be under the circumstances, with many teachers working in their classrooms and a few students hanging around in the high school. The girls' soccer team was practicing on the sports field, while the boys had gone off campus to practice in Joli Bois, an area south of central Waterloo. Several staff members were already anticipating what might be happening in the near-term future and asked if there would be school tomorrow. At this time, the honest answer was, "I don't know."

It was 5:15 p.m. as I swung by the secondary library for another news update from the television. The North Tower of the World Trade Center had now also collapsed, and video was being shown of that, as well as of the earlier footage of the planes crashing and the South Tower collapsing. It was time to get back to the office for Mike Valle's next phone call, so I started moving in that direction. As I walked past the reception area in front of a wall mural of Pope John XXIII, about a dozen of the cross country team members were entering the building after returning from a workout at the Château de la Hulpe. The coaches normally drove them in a school van to the château grounds after school. It was an ideal location for running on the many hiking trails through the woods. After the workout, the coaches would drive back and drop off the kids in front of the school before parking the vehicles in the underground garage.

As they entered the building, the kids were laughing and horsing around, obviously oblivious to what was happening in the United States. I stopped them and asked if they were aware of the news about airplanes crashing into buildings in New York and Washington. Suddenly their demeanor changed as they seemed to realize the enormous consequences of the events underway. One of the girls asked if there would be school tomorrow. Again I responded, "I don't know."

Everyone had already gone home from the villa when I returned about 5:30 p.m. Mike Valle soon phoned again from the embassy. This time he was more direct in making a recommendation and in getting straight to the point. "Joe, I think you should cancel school tomorrow. It's better to be safe than sorry until we figure out what's going on." I did not hesitate in responding, "If you say we should cancel school, then that's what we'll do. I'm not about to disregard your advice under these circumstances." We agreed to speak again tomorrow morning, but to phone one another at home if any news developed overnight.

Suddenly the logistical wheels were turning, and I felt like I was doing something in response to the crisis. My first step was to phone Alain Fastre, who was president of the school advisory board. Alain was Belgian and a Nokia executive. He was totally aware of what was happening and immediately concurred with my decision to cancel school tomorrow. My next phone call was to Sr. Barbara Hughes, FCJ, my predecessor as head of the school. She was living in the convent in Brussels and was also on the advisory board. I wanted to keep the sisters in the loop on all important decisions, and Sr. Barbara was the key contact, given her previous role and her ongoing involvement with school activities.

My next move was to phone Kevin Bartlett, the director of the International School of Brussels (ISB). Kevin was new on the job, having just arrived a few weeks earlier from Namibia, where he was director of the Windhoek International School. ISB was the other major international school in the Brussels area. Like St. John's, it had a large contingent of Americans. The two schools were friendly rivals, competing for the same pool of international students while also competing in sports activities. There was a third "international" school in the Brussels area, the British School of Brussels (BSB), but it had only a handful of Americans and drew most of its enrollment from the Commonwealth Nations. Despite the rivalry, ISB and St. John's enjoyed a positive professional relationship. As a courtesy we would traditionally contact one another when one or the other made a decision to cancel school. This would usually happen once or twice a year in the winter when snow or ice would make it too dangerous to run the school buses.

I reached Kevin's secretary, who was still on the job despite it being almost 6:00 p.m. She knew immediately why I was calling. Kevin picked up the line within a few seconds. I wasted no time on pleasantries and went straight to the point. "Kevin, we have been advised by the American Embassy to close tomorrow, and that's what we're going to do." Kevin immediately concurred, and we agreed to stay in touch. The whole conversation lasted less than two minutes.

Finally, I phoned the three principals and confirmed that there would be no classes tomorrow. They must have anticipated such a decision, as all of them were ready to activate their phone tree. This was a system that we had in place to notify everyone of important decisions when it was not possible to do so during normal school hours. I triggered the phone tree at the top by calling the principals. They then phoned their department leaders or grade-level coordinators, who in turn notified the classroom teachers. At this point in the phone tree all of the staff were informed. The classroom teachers finished it out by phoning every parent for the students in their classroom at the elementary level or every parent of each student in their advisory group for middle and high school. Naturally, the information would go viral as soon as the first few parents got the word and the students started calling one another. In addition, I notified Jean-Louis Cornez, our technology coordinator, who posted the information on the school website.

As I was about to leave the office around 6:30, the phone rang. I answered immediately, thinking that it might be the embassy again. It was Yves Vander Cruysen, the premier échevin, or right-hand man, of the mayor on the Waterloo city council. We spoke in a mixture of English and French, as he wanted to emphasize that the commune of Waterloo was prepared to help St. John's in any way. I thanked him for his concern, let him know that we had already canceled school for tomorrow, and said that I would get back in touch if we needed anything. It was certainly a nice and much appreciated gesture on the part of the city officials. We were not in this alone.

At 6:45 I turned off all the lights in the villa, locked the front door, and set the alarm system before walking across the lawn to the crosswalk. While I waited for the light to change, cars were streaming past in both directions. It was still daylight, but the sun was getting low in the sky and a soft drizzle was falling. Finally the stop light came on, the vehicles stopped, and I scurried across the street with a wave to the drivers.

The buildings were still open, as the cleaning crew were going through the routine of sweeping, mopping, and emptying the trash. It took about two minutes to walk through the ground floor of the elementary wing, followed by the high school wing, across the foyer of the middle school, and down the stairs past my wife's science lab in the basement. I then walked into the underground parking area next to the middle school science labs.

Within minutes I was out of the garage and turning right on Dréve Richelle to drive home, only three kilometers from the school. Martha had already gone home and was waiting with another middle school teacher, Monica Smith, who insisted on staying with her until I arrived. I immediately joined them in front of the television which was tuned to the cable news in English. Switching back and forth between CNN and Sky News, I was glued to the screen and could not get enough of it, even though everything was basically a repeat of what had been shown earlier, interspersed with political commentary from both sides of the Atlantic.

Monica left and Martha prepared a quick meal, which we ate while still watching the news. At 10:00 p.m. we were both exhausted from the emotional stress of the day and went upstairs to bed, where we fell into a deep sleep.

CHAPTER 4

September 12, 2001

I awoke as usual at 5:00 a.m. and lay in bed reflecting on yesterday's events for about ten minutes before getting up and putting on a sweat suit and running shoes. I added a reflector vest to increase my visibility to passing motorists. Stepping outside and crossing the street, I noticed that it was dry and a little warmer than yesterday. It was still dark and not possible to determine how clear or cloudy it might be. I began my morning ritual of jogging on the sidewalk along the Chaussée de Louvain toward La Hulpe. There were cornfields on my left and houses on the right as I slowly jogged for about fifteen minutes and then crossed the street to return on the other side. The darkness and morning stillness provided a good environment for reflecting on yesterday's events and for requesting Divine strength and guidance to get through all of the uncertainty. During the entire half hour of jogging only five or six vehicles passed me. Back home, I lifted weights in the garage for another fifteen minutes before cleaning up, getting dressed, and grabbing a quick bite to eat.

It was a few minutes after 7:00 a.m. when I left home and headed for the school. Martha stayed home since classes had been canceled. She could keep up with the unending task of grading papers and planning lessons from home just as easily as being in her classroom. I parked on the street next to the villa instead of in the underground garage. After entering the office and dropping off my briefcase, I walked across the street to the school.

There did not seem to be anyone on campus, other than the concierges who lived on the grounds, one in an apartment next to the secondary library, one in a small house in the Timber Tops preschool complex, and a third in a house next to the cafeteria. Before I could enter the main building, a Waterloo police car pulled into the driveway with two officers. There was no forewarning of their arrival, but they were in uniform and obviously on an official mission. I wondered if perhaps they had been parked, watching and waiting until someone arrived. Speaking in French and assuming that I was someone with authority, they asked if they could inspect the buildings. Of course I agreed and led them into the elementary wing, which had three levels. Rather than stay with them, I returned to the reception area and the main school entry. After twenty minutes, they returned and commented that everything looked normal.

They wanted to check the high school wing next, so I showed them the layout of the building. The bottom level consisted of fourth- and fifth-grade classrooms. It was known as B-level. The next floor consisted of high school English classrooms and was known as C-level. The top floor contained the science labs and was known as D-level. Using traditional American terminology to designate different floors in an international school would have been confusing. First floor and ground floor mean the same thing for an American, but not for a European. Consequently the school used the alphabet to designate levels, with A being the bottom and D being the fourth, or top.

The two officers stayed on D-level, and I returned to the main entrance once again. Within five minutes they returned and said that there was a suspicious backpack in the hallway on C-level. They called for assistance and we waited. Soon a police van arrived with three more officers. I was relieved that they parked quietly in the driveway, as sirens and flashing lights would have served no useful purpose under the circumstances. All five officers then helped unload a large mechanical device from the back of the van. It looked at first glance like a riding lawnmower but was obviously a bomb-retrieving robot that resembled a small bulldozer with long mechanical arms. The device was battery powered and moved on tracks that were about a meter long on both sides.

Four of the officers muscled the device up off the ground, carried it through the front door, and ascended the steps. The fifth stayed at the entry to prevent anyone from going inside. I remained with him to turn away anyone who might try to enter. My thoughts were that some of the teachers might try to get into the building with the hope of working uninterrupted in the classroom. Some teachers avoided the campus at all costs when school was not in session, but many of them loved to spend time in their classroom when no one else was around to disturb them. It was productive preparation time.

After an hour and a half, the officers returned with the robot and said that the buildings were all clear. The backpack contained an empty lunch pail and some blank papers. There was no name to identify the owner. It was both an emotional and a physical relief to hear their comments. Most important, I was relieved that they found no bombs, which would have elevated the police response to unimaginable levels and drawn the attention of the local and international media. I was also physically relieved because I was tired of standing and pacing back and forth the past two hours. The robot was lifted back into the van, and all five officers left in their two vehicles.

At this point it was 11:00 a.m. when I returned to the villa across the street and phoned Mike Valle at the U.S. Embassy. I informed him of the police inspection and the robot's visit. He seemed impressed that the Waterloo police would be so responsive. According to the embassy intelligence data, things were starting to settle down in New York and Washington. There was nothing to suggest that any terror activity was imminent in Belgium. Nevertheless, he warned that it was necessary to be cautious in the days ahead. It was possible that local extremists might try to target an institution with a large American presence such as St. John's.

Next we discussed the reopening of school. If he did not have a good reason for staying closed, I wanted to resume classes tomorrow and get back into a normal routine sooner rather than later. Mike had no objections, so we agreed that classes would resume on Thursday, September 13. I communicated this to the principals and phoned Kevin Bartlett at ISB. He was also planning to have school tomorrow. Jean-Louis Cornez then updated the St. John's website to announce the resumption of classes on Thursday. We did not activate the phone tree as we did on Tuesday, sticking with the idea that we called only to cancel school. The informal communication network was also in full motion. Nadine had come in and was answering one phone call after another regarding tomorrow. She also phoned the bus companies that transported our students in order to make sure that the normal pick-up schedule would be in effect tomorrow morning.

There was a lull in the action at 1:00 p.m., so I left the villa, crossed the street, and walked to Longbois Bakery, about a hundred meters past the school. I bought a sandwich and returned to the villa to eat it while waiting for anything to occur unexpectedly. For the next three hours, I answered several phone calls from staff members and from parents, assuring everyone that it was safe to resume classes tomorrow. At 4:30 I turned out the lights, locked the villa, set the alarm, and drove home to watch the television news. Sitting around and waiting for tomorrow made me feel uneasy. I had the feeling that there must be something I should be doing to be better prepared for what might happen in the morning. With the television still tuned to CNN, I started reading the *International Herald Tribune* before getting sleepy and going to bed.

CHAPTER 5

September 13, 2001

A light rain was falling as I left the house for my regular morning jog. The exercise routine was the same as usual, and my mind began to conjure up a pessimistic scenario that perhaps I was being watched. I always left the house about 5:15 a.m., crossed the street, and jogged toward La Hulpe. In other words, my Monday through Friday early morning exercise was very predictable. If someone wanted to follow my movements and do me harm, it would be easy to do so at that time of day. It was dark. A car might pass every eight minutes or so. The cornfields provided an excellent place to hide, wait, and watch without being seen. Hence, I was on full alert as I made my way along the chaussée and back home.

Martha and I left the house earlier than usual and arrived at school at 7:15 a.m. Sharing one car meant that we went almost everywhere together. She didn't seem to mind because it gave her extra time in both the mornings and evenings to work in her classroom, setting up labs, grading papers, and preparing lessons. Our parking space in the underground garage was only a twenty-second walk from her classroom.

As we turned left into the campus from Dréve Richelle, I noticed several people in uniform standing in front of the school. Anxiety set in as I hurriedly parked the car, climbed the stairs from A-level, and walked through the halls to the reception area where I had seen the people in uniform. The campus was still almost totally deserted, as the buses didn't start to arrive until about eight o'clock and the bell to start first period didn't sound until 8:30.

A group of Belgian federal police officers were standing around talking. I knew immediately that these were not local Waterloo officers because of the way they were dressed. No one had told me that the police would be on campus. Their presence was a total surprise, but not a shock under the circumstances. It made me wonder what they knew that I did not know. Did they have intelligence information that local extremists might try to terrorize St. John's because it was a soft target with lots of American students? Ignorance can sometimes be bliss, and certainly that was the case until about two minutes ago. Had I known yesterday that the federal police would be on campus today, I would not have slept well last night.

Despite all of the uncertainty, I was pleased to see their presence, as it definitely added a layer of security. I introduced myself to the officer-in-charge. Most of the conversation was in French, which was possible only because I was now in my fourth year of lessons at a local language school. The commander assured me that there was no imminent threat and that they would not enter the buildings unless requested. Their plan was to constantly patrol the outdoor areas around the campus perimeter. With the sports fields, parking areas, and buildings, it was about a one-kilometer walk around the entire complex.

There were three teams of two officers dressed in full combat gear, including flak jackets. One officer in each team controlled a bomb-sniffing dog on a leash while the second officer carried some kind of automatic rifle with a shoulder strap and the barrel pointed down at the ground, but in the ready position with hand next to the trigger housing. Hence, there were a total of seven police, counting the leader, and three dogs. Two of the officers were women.

I excused myself and indicated that I would be back in few minutes. At this point the only students on campus were the children of staff members, who were just now starting to arrive. With the officers and dogs still standing in the driveway, I hurried across the street to the villa and immediately phoned Mike Valle at the American Embassy. He was not aware that the federal police had been deployed to the campus but seemed pleased with this development. We agreed to stay in touch, and I headed back across street to the school.

At this point, the first bus of the day was arriving. As it passed in front of the school, many of the riders were staring out the windows at the police and their dogs. One could feel the sense of excitement that comes with a mixture of youthful exuberance and naïveté. The remaining buses soon arrived, and parents dropped off children as they always did. When the bells sounded at 8:30, the campus seemed to be back in a normal routine with no indication that parents were keeping children home from school. The attendance rate was the same as for a normal Thursday.

Meanwhile, the police officers and dogs were patrolling the grounds. The commander left, but the three teams spread out and walked around the campus all day long. Basically it was a show of force and a gesture of support for the international community in Waterloo. Fortunately, it was boring work with nothing out of the ordinary to draw their attention. I never spoke to the officers, other than to nod hello, but they were very professional and highly visible. The dogs certainly added a dimension that got everyone's attention. When the buses departed at the end of the day, most of the students were gone and most of the teachers were in the process of leaving. The police officers and dogs stopped patrolling about five minutes after the final bus departed at 3:50 p.m. Within minutes they left in three vehicles. I had no idea what their plans were for tomorrow. It was wait and see.

As I reflected on the day, it was an amazing experience. We were able to carry out our educational mission, but in a setting that was totally bizarre. I wondered what Marie Madeleine d'Houët would have thought about the whole scene. The foundress of the Faithful Companions of Jesus was a visionary committed to the Christian education of children. Surely she was aware of the traumatic effects of violence since she began her work in the aftermath of the French Revolution. The guillotine was in common use then, and Napoleon was launching one military campaign after another. Ironically, one of the most brutal battles in the history of warfare occurred a mere five kilometers from the St. John's campus. More than forty thousand troops were killed or wounded during the Battle of Waterloo. Nevertheless, there we were: an FCJ international school serving more than one thousand children from sixty different countries being guarded by heavily armed police officers and bomb-sniffing dogs.

CHAPTER 6

September 14 through September 18, 2001

The police patrols continued on Friday, September 14, and returned again on Monday. Each day brought the same routine. They would arrive about 7:00 a.m., walk around the buildings and grounds all day long, and leave about 4:00 p.m. By Monday, their presence had become part of the daily routine. The novelty had worn off. Everyone seemed used to their presence. Never even once was there any kind of incident to trigger a response. The dogs were well trained and simply followed their handlers' directions. A few students tried to interact with the animals, but the officers professionally discouraged such behavior. All in all, the police and the dogs seemed a bit bored with their monotonous duty, but they were always polite and ready with a smile. With all of their weapons and tactical training, they probably never anticipated being assigned to guard a school.

The weekend of September 15 and 16 was quiet. The weather was typical for the time of year. Saturday was partly cloudy with periods of sunshine. Sunday had on- and off-again rain showers, but nothing heavy. I drove to the school both days just to walk around. Everything was normal. The three live-in concierges, Jacques, Mark, and Paolo, reported nothing unusual.

On Monday, September 17, the police returned again and settled into their patrol routine. Shortly after 9:00 a.m. I was confronted by two Swedish mothers as I crossed the street from the villa to the school. It was one of those spontaneous interactions that occur without warning. They aggressively informed me that the police and dogs were scaring their children. From their perspective, there was no place for such a frightening experience in a school. They demanded that I remove the police and dogs immediately.

I was speechless for a moment while trying to read their facial expressions to determine if this was some kind of joke. Realizing the seriousness of their comments, I collected my thoughts and tried to appear calm in telling them that "security is our top priority, and the police will stay as long as the Belgian authorities think it is necessary." I forced a smile and tried to reassure them that I understood their concerns but that they must try to understand mine. They walked away not happy, but seemingly satisfied that they had been able to speak their mind. The next day, Tuesday, September 18, the police patrols did not return. This occurred without notification. They simply did not show up in the morning. No one phoned to warn me of the pending withdrawal or to check on things after the fact. When I phoned Mike Valle at the embassy, he had no information either. So I just let the matter drop. We didn't ask for the patrols in the first place, and we didn't ask for them to be discontinued. Nevertheless, we certainly appreciated the support at a time of crisis when no one knew what to expect. I could not help but think that those same parents who complained might have taken their case to Belgian officials.

After school on Tuesday, Daniel Mies, the school messenger who handled all of the mail, approached me as I was walking down the corridor in the elementary wing. The buildings were empty except for the cleaning crew, which was busy sweeping and mopping. Daniel was a slim, tall man of about fifty who would do anything for anybody. It was an inspiration to see how Daniel and his wife cared for a disabled son with such love and attention. Daniel had a stressful look on his face as he asked me to follow him. We went outside to the old FCJ mailbox in front of the school. It was built into the stone pillar next to the entrance driveway.

He opened the mailbox and pointed inside. There was a legal-size envelope with some sort of white powder spilling out of it. Daniel pointed inside the box, and I immediately recognized his concern. Was this a terror attack with anthrax powder? I said nothing for at least thirty seconds while running through all of the possibilities in my mind. If I called the police, there would most likely be a full-scale response with sirens and flashing lights, much to the delight of whoever placed the envelope in the mailbox. On the other hand, if it was not anthrax and I disposed of it myself, that would most likely be the end of the story. Realizing that my time for contemplation had been exhausted, I reached into the mailbox and, very uncomfortably, grabbed the envelope. I slid it out and held it up to inspect the contents while Daniel watched. It seemed rather obvious that the contents were either flour or powdered sugar. My thinking was that if it were anthrax, the volume would be less and it would be much better contained in the envelope. Instead, it was spilling out so that whoever prepared it must have gotten it on themselves and their clothes. I thanked Daniel for bringing it to my attention and tried to look calm as I walked back to the large trash bins behind the school where I disposed of the envelope and its contents.

CHAPTER 7

The Aftermath

Classes soon returned to a more normal routine, but everyone realized that things would never be the same again. Schools were soft targets for terrorists, and international schools were especially attractive because of the heavy diplomatic presence. Hence, a discomforting sense of unease lingered as we wondered how vulnerable we might be. The situation in the States rapidly stabilized, and the source of the attacks was quickly identified as Bin Laden and his followers working out of Afghanistan. This knowledge removed some of the uncertainty.

The culture of St. John's, however, was very open and tolerant with a commitment to fairness. Hence, the many Muslim families from Saudi Arabia, Pakistan, and Bangladesh felt very comfortable in a caring environment where Christian values were emphasized. They chose St. John's with full knowledge of the school's ethos and certainly seemed happy with the setting in which the children were being educated. There was never any internal tension. I cannot recall a single instance of conflict among the students or parents related to September 11.

Nevertheless, pretending that the terror attacks in the United States did not happen or ignoring the fact that armed guards patrolled the St. John's campus for three days was not an option. We could not continue on with business as usual. Security had now risen to the top of the priority list.

My first effort was to develop an evacuation plan should we receive a bomb threat. Moving one thousand students outside to rendezvous points, as we did for fire drills, was not an adequate plan. Fire drills lasted only fifteen minutes and could be timed to avoid the frequent Belgian rain. Leaving the buildings for an extended period of time was a much more complex matter.

I began by meeting with the director of Berlaymont, a Belgian school in Waterloo. It had a large campus that bordered the forest and was located about 1.5 kilometers from St. John's. The director was very understanding and kind as she offered her school as a "refugee" center if it ever became necessary to evacuate

St. John's during the school day. She even emphasized that her food service staff would be able to feed our students if we had to bring them to Berlaymont during the school day.

The plan was to take all of the first through fifth graders to Berlaymont by walking under the supervision of the elementary teachers and support staff. The primary evacuation route was to cross Dréve Richelle and walk down the street past the villa and proceed toward the Waterloo sewage plant. At this point the pavement stopped and the children would have to walk through the woods to reach Berlaymont. This was the shortest route and the safest because there was no traffic to worry about. We also needed an alternate route if it were too muddy to walk through the woods. The second route was longer and more dangerous because of the traffic. It involved crossing Dréve Richelle and walking west past the office park before turning north and continuing on the sidewalk of the Chaussée de Tervuren.

With the elementary school taken care of, I next met with the director of Sainte-Anne's school in the Joli Bois area of Waterloo. He, too, was very understanding and cooperative. We were welcome to use his school as an evacuation point, with the church and gymnasium serving as the two hosting sites. The plan was once again to walk the 1.5-kilometer distance by following the sidewalk along the ring road, under the overpass, and into the Joli Bois neighborhood. This route was paved all the way with roads and sidewalks. All of the middle and high school students would follow this route accompanied by their teachers.

That left the preschool children from Timber Tops. The three-, four- and five-year-olds would obviously require more supervision. Since there were only about a hundred of them, we made arrangements to move them to a couple of private homes in the residential neighborhood surrounding the villa. It was only about a five-minute walk from the school. Both homes were large with spacious lawn and garden areas. Both were also occupied by St. John's families who were happy to assist. One belonged to the school business manager, Rick Katherman.

I did not want to dwell on the possibility of having to evacuate St. John's, but at least there was a plan in place to do so in a worst-case scenario. Right or wrong, we had never thought about such an event prior to September 11.

CHAPTER 8

Security Upgrades

In the aftermath of September 11, we immediately increased our security precautions with local initiatives such as electronic door locks, traffic barriers, and check-in procedures with visitor's passes. The electronic door locks were almost too effective, as they locked the three primary entrance points with an automatic timer. This led to students, parents, and even some staff members propping open the doors with a chair or some other object in order to keep them from locking while they were on the outside if they wanted to get back inside. Hence, the door security was much better, but few people embraced the inconvenience. Meanwhile the traffic barriers required those wishing to drive on campus to punch in a code before the barrier would rise to allow the vehicle to pass. This system led to frequent comical scenarios when staff members would pull up too far from the code keyboard. In such instances they would have to hang out the window of the car to punch in the code or back up and try to pull closer if no one was waiting behind them. One can imagine the stress experienced by a teacher who pulls up to the barrier, but is not close enough to reach the keyboard after rolling down the window. If someone else had pulled in behind them and was waiting, backing up and starting over was not an option. Typically the driver's door was too close to the pillar upon which the keyboard was mounted. Hence getting out of the car was almost impossible. This meant unfastening one's seatbelt and leaning out the window. Naturally the inconvenience was elevated in poor weather and especially in the rain.

The major security upgrades, however, took several years to complete, plus the financial support of the American Embassy. Within a year of the September 11 catastrophe, the U.S. State Department began sponsoring security grants for international schools with large American enrollments. About 30 percent of our students were from the United States. Hence, some three hundred kids carried American passports. The embassy in Brussels suggested that St. John's apply.

As soon as the documentation was released, I immediately began to work on the application process.

It was typical federal paperwork with lengthy forms to complete. I made it my top priority because I was afraid that the allocation of funds would be insufficient for all of the schools that would apply. If the St. John's application were submitted to Washington as soon as possible, then we might get the grant money before the International School of Brussels. If there was enough funding for only one school in Belgium, perhaps we would get it. Fortunately, our grant application was approved, and we moved quickly to select contractors for the work. Despite our efforts to submit the grant application as fast as possible, it still took three years to wind through the federal bureaucracy and receive final approval.

During the summer of 2005, shatter-resistant film was applied on all exterior windows. At the same time, a school-wide intercom system was installed throughout the campus. The film was designed to prevent the glass from shattering in the event of an explosion. The intercom system allowed for instant communication from the school and villa offices to anywhere on campus. Obviously, the intercom provided more than an emergency communication system, as there were no restrictions on using it for daily announcements. The cost of these two security features was approximately

$350,000. ISB eventually received a similar grant, but St. John's was first.

A year later, another round of security funding was released by Washington for international schools with substantial American populations. Once again St. John's applied immediately and was awarded another $350,000. The main feature was an eight-foot-tall iron security fence that ran around the entire perimeter of the campus. It included five electronic gates that were connected to the reception desk and controlled by the person on duty. In addition to the fence, the grant also paid for sixteen surveillance cameras strategically placed both inside and outside the buildings, along with video monitors to observe the camera coverage areas. Erection of the fence and installation of cameras took place from October through December 2007. Like the intercom system that served the school for more than just security, the cameras and video system had multiple uses. The video images were dated, timed, and stored for two weeks. Hence, it was possible to check the video if something happened that needed to be reviewed. Parking lot fender benders and occasional acts of vandalism could now be investigated with state-of-the-art security equipment.

Everyone loved the idea of the shatter-resistant windows, the usefulness of the intercom system, and the practicality of the surveillance cameras. However, not everyone was pleased with the fence. The students didn't seem to care one way or the other, but I received several complaints from teachers and parents. The primary gripe was that the fence was ugly and made the school look like a prison. As the saying goes, "beauty is in the eye of the beholder." For most people the fence was just fine and did not detract from the attractiveness of the campus. For a few it was an unwelcome addition to the learning environment. For everyone it represented a new reality for post–September 11, 2001. Not even schools could afford to ignore the potential threat of terrorism. A perimeter fence, ugly or not, did indeed restrict access to the school while also controlling departures by the high school students who liked to walk down the street to the Delhaize deli and grocery to buy snacks during break time or lunch.

I conclude this true story of the 9/11 experience at St. John's with a humorous anecdote about the opening of the Performing Arts Center over Thanksgiving weekend in November 2005. As an international school with students from sixty different countries, St. John's did not observe a Thanksgiving holiday weekend in Waterloo. Nevertheless, with three hundred American students, there was an awareness of the event, and many American parents would come to school to visit on that Thursday because they did have the holiday at their place of employment. It was on this weekend that we decided to have the first performance in the newly constructed and state-of-the-art theater. The drama and music departments collaborated on producing *The Sound of Music,* which seemed like the right show at the right time in the right place, given the Christian ethos of St. John's and its ongoing history with the FCJ sisters. Cathy Swanson, the music program coordinator, and Alan Hayes, the theater teacher, both enthusiastically bought into the idea and did a superb job of making it a memorable experience.

I invited Tom Korologos, the U.S. ambassador to the Kingdom of Belgium. He had already visited St. John's several times and had even joined the students for lunch in the school cafeteria, along with his wife, Ann McLaughlin Korologos. They immediately accepted the invitation, and we prepared to host them for the opening performance on Friday, November 25, the day after Thanksgiving.

Ambassador Korologos was originally from Utah, but he had a consulting business in Washington, where he was an advisor to presidents, senators, and congressmen. President Bush sent him to Baghdad in 2003 to serve as a counselor for the Coalition Provisional Authority in Iraq. This assignment preceded his appointment as ambassador in Brussels. Hence, he was quite sensitive to the necessity for security. His wife, Ann, had a very distinguished career in her own right. She had previously served as the U.S. Secretary of Labor under Ronald Reagan.

Ambassador and Mrs. Korologos arrived about 7:00 p.m., thirty minutes before the performance was scheduled to begin. They were accompanied by four security officers, two of whom sat in the row and seats immediately behind him and two of whom stood on opposite sides of the theater against the wall and facing the four hundred people in attendance. All four were wired with ear pieces and small lapel microphones. We were engaged in small talk when, about ten minutes before curtain time, Ambassador Korologos asked where the men's room was located. Instead of pointing him to the public restrooms in the foyer, I asked him to follow me upstairs where I knew that there would be no one else using the facility. Ann stayed in the theater and continued chatting with Martha.

We walked out of the theater accompanied by one of the security officers and crossed the side lobby to the elevator. I pushed the button, the door soon opened, and the three of us stepped inside. The doors closed as we continued talking about the construction of the theater. We were totally focused on our conversation when suddenly the lights went out. It was pitch black inside the elevator as the security officer began speaking into his lapel microphone to his colleagues and calling for backup. I was almost sick to my stomach thinking that either we had just lost power on opening night or, worse, a terrorist kidnapping was under way involving the American ambassador. Then suddenly I realized that perhaps I had not pushed the button on the control panel. I reached over in the darkness, found the panel, fumbled around until I found buttons, and pushed the one to go upstairs. The lights came on immediately, the elevator started to ascend, and we all breathed a sigh of relief. I apologized. He laughed. The security officer alerted his partner to stand down.

The show was a huge success with Ambassador Korologos commenting that it was as good as anything he had seen on the West End of London or Broadway in New York. When we walked outside afterward to meet his driver and car, it was snowing hard. It had not been snowing long enough to create dangerous driving conditions, but long enough to cover the lawns and trees with a beautiful white coat that glistened in the lights. It almost seemed as if we were being blessed with manna from heaven, a symbolic gesture that St. John's would continue to thrive and carry out its mission in a new post–9/11 world.

As this memoir of September 11, 2001, is being published, St. John's International School is celebrating its fiftieth anniversary. Half a century has gone by since the FCJs responded to the request from the international business community to begin an English-speaking school anchored in Christian values for the children of expats in Belgium. Priceless memories have been created over the years for thousands of students and families. Many events with global impact occurred during these five decades: the election and attempted assassination of a Polish pope; the destruction of the Berlin Wall and the disintegration of the Soviet Union; the Gulf War and the liberation of Kuwait; the fall of Apartheid and the rise of democracy in South Africa. Nothing, however, matches the impact of what happened on September 11, 2001. The terror attacks in New York and Washington changed the world. St. John's International School was dramatically affected by events four thousand miles away but emerged from the experience with a greater appreciation of its history and a renewed determination to continue its legacy. Those of us who lived through it will never forget.

ABOUT THE AUTHOR

Joe Doenges has bachelor's and master's degrees from the University of Texas at Austin and a doctor's degree from Texas Tech. His career in education includes roles as a teacher, coach, assistant principal, principal, and superintendent. He previously published "Books and Butts" and resides in Florida. His wife, Martha, passed away in 2021.